an Allergan handbook

Management of

Ocular Emergencies

Raymond Stein, M.D., FRCSC
Harold Stein, M.D., FRCSC
Bernard Slatt, M.D., FRCSC

 Medicöpea

Canadian Cataloguing in Publication Data

Stein, Raymond
Management of ocular emergencies

"An Allergan Handbook"
ISBN 0-919821-18-9

1. Ophthalmologic emergencies. 2. Eye Diseases and defects. I. Stein, Harold A. (Harold Aaron), 1929 - II. Slatt, Bernard, 1934 - III. Title.

RE48.9.S83   1990   617.7'1   C90-090300-7

Applications and usage
    The authors and publisher have exerted every effort to insure that the application and use of all drugs, devices, and procedures mentioned in this publication are in accord with current recommendations and practices. However, in view of ongoing research, changes in regulations, and the constant flow of information relating to ophthalmology, the reader is cautioned to consult the package insert of any product for the approved indications and dosage recommendations in Canada as well as for the incidences of adverse reactions and mortality.

All Rights Reserved

Copyright © 1990. All rights reserved. No part of this book may be reproduced or transmitted in any form by any means, electronic or mechanical, including photocopying, recording, or by any information storage and retrieval system, without permission in writing from the authors.

Prepared, printed, and published in Montreal, Canada, by:
Medicöpea International Inc.
212-8200, Decarie Boulevard
Montreal, Canada H4P 2P5
Copyright 1990
ISBN 0-919821-18-9

CONTENTS

Introduction

This manual is designed to be a practical guide to the management of ocular emergencies, and presents the clinical principles used in our everyday ophthalmic practice. The material arose from a series of lectures given to emergency room physcians, medical students, and ophthalmology residents, and was enthusiastically received for its simplified approach and organization.

An attempt has been made to organize the material into clinically relevant sections. The first section highlights the essentials of the eye examination. The second section deals with the emergency ocular diseases, and is divided into those diseases in which the patient presents with either a red eye or a white eye. The red eye conditions are those that may be nontraumatic or secondary to trauma; the white eye conditions are those that are associated with a decrease in vision or diplopia. The final section contains a series of tables that may be helpful for the differential diagnosis of a variety of emergency cases.

We hope that this manual will serve as a useful guide to the clinician for the management of ocular emergencies.

Raymond M. Stein, M.D., FRCSC
Harold A. Stein, M.D., FRCSC
Bernard Slatt, M.D., FRCSC

Ocular History and Examination

INTRODUCTION
The type and characteristics of the presenting symptoms can often suggest a provisional diagnosis prior to the examination. The nature of the symptoms should be recorded, including any precipitating factors, and whether the episode is recurrent, constant or intermittent, and whether the onset was gradual or acute. Common symptoms include decreased vision, redness, photophobia, tearing, itching, foreign body sensation, burning, pain, and diplopia.

A brief medical history should be obtained. A variety of systemic diseases can affect the eye, including diabetes mellitus, hypertension, thyroid disease, rheumatoid arthritis, cancer (Appendices A, B). All medications should be documented, as certain systemic medications can cause ocular symptoms (Appendix C). Drug allergies should be determined before eye drops are instilled or medications prescribed. Any family history of ocular diseases should be recorded.

An examination should then be conducted, and should include a test of visual acuity, pupils, motility, confrontation visual field, the anterior segment, the posterior segment, and intraocular pressure.

VISUAL ACUITY
Check the distance visual acuity (VA) for each eye. This is usually performed at 20 feet (6 meters) using letters, numbers, or an illiterate E chart. In order of best to worst vision, acuities recorded are as follows: 20/15, 20/20, 20/25, 20/30, 20/40, 20/50, 20/60, 20/70, 20/80, 20/100, 20/200, 20/400, counting fingers, hand movements, light perception, and no light perception. If a patient has a VA of 20/60, this means that he sees at 20 feet what a normal person sees at 60 feet. Similary, a VA of 20/15 means that he sees at 20 feet what a normal person sees at 15 feet.

Near vision is usually checked with a reading card held at 14 inches. This is the most convenient way to check vision in the hospitalized patient.

If the patient has corrective lenses, they should be worn during testing. The examiner must try to determine optimum acuity. If the vision is less than 20/20, the potential for improved vision should be ascertained by having the patient look through a pinhole. Improved vision with a pinhole indicates that appropriate glasses or contact lenses would be beneficial; unimproved vision suggests that a nonrefractive problem such as corneal edema, cataracts, or macular degeneration may exist. Visual acuity should be checked in both eyes since some patients are unaware of an amblyopic eye. If the good eye of such a patient is patched, he may be at serious risk of a motor vehicle accident when he drives.

PUPILS
The pupillary size and reaction to light stimulation should be checked, carefully noting the presence of a dilated or constricted pupil. The swinging flashlight test is used to determine the absence or presence of an afferent pupillary defect.

During the swinging flashlight test the examiner projects the light on the right eye (for example), allowing the right pupil to constrict to a minimum size and subsequently escape to an intermediate size. The light is then quickly swung to the left eye, which constricts from an intermediate to a minimum size, subsequently escaping to an intermediate size. At this point the light is swung again to the right eye and a mental note is made of the intermediate (starting) pupil size and briskness of the response to light. These characteristics should be exactly the same in both eyes as the light is alternately swung to each eye.

Afferent Pupillary Defect

The swinging flashlight test will determine if the amount of light transmitted from one eye is less than that carried via the fellow eye; when the light is swung to the defective eye, immediate dilatation of the pupil occurs instead of the normal initial constriction. This characterizes an afferent pupillary defect. The differential diagnosis includes a retinal detachment, occlusion of a central retinal artery or vein, optic neuritis or optic neuropathy.

N.B.: Cataract, hyphema, vitreous hemorrhage, corneal ulcer, and iritis are associated with a decrease in vision, but are *not associated with an afferent pupillary defect.*

Differential Diagnosis of a Dilated Pupil

A dilated pupil may be due to third nerve palsy, trauma, Adie's pupil, acute glaucoma, or may be drug-induced.

Third Nerve Palsy. If the dilated pupil is fixed, the cause may be third nerve palsy. This condition may be associated with ptosis and a motility disturbance, characterized by the eye being deviated out and down. The pupil responds to constricting drops, e.g., pilocarpine. This is a neurosurgical emergency, as the possibility of an intracranial mass lesion must be ruled out.

Trauma. Damage to the iris sphincter may result from a blunt or penetrating injury. Iris transillumination defects may be visible with the ophthalmoscope or slit lamp, and the pupil may have an irregular shape.

Adie's Pupil. The pupil responds better to near stimulation than to light. The condition is thought to be related to aberrant innervation of the iris by axons which normally stimulate the ciliary body.

Drug-Induced. Iatrogenic or self-contamination may occur with a variety of dilating drops, e.g., Cyclogyl®, Mydriacyl®, homatropine, scopalamine, atropine. The pupil is fixed and dilated and, unlike in third nerve palsy, does not respond to constricting drops.

Acute Glaucoma. The patient may complain of pain and/or nausea and vomiting. The eye is red, the vision is diminished, the intraocular pressure is elevated, and the pupil is mid-dilated and poorly reactive.

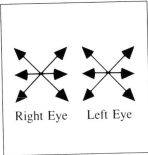

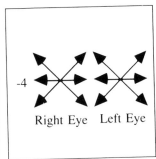

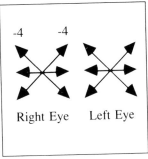

Fig. 1 Method for examining and recording ocular motiliy

Fig. 2 Record of a sixth nerve palsy of the right eye

Fig. 3 Record of a right orbital blow-out fracture and limited upgaze

Differential Diagnosis of a Constricted Pupil

A constriced pupil occurs in Horner's syndrome, iritis, and may be drug-induced.

Horner's Syndrome. Other signs of this condition include mild ptosis of the upper lid and retraction of the lower lid. The difference in pupillary size is more notable in dim light since adrenergic innervation to the iris dilator muscle is diminished.

Drug-Induced. Iatrogenic or self-induced pupillary constriction may be due to a variety of drugs, including pilocarpine, carbachol, and Phospholine iodide®.

Iritis. Slit lamp examination shows keratic precipitates and cells in the anterior chamber, and there is a prominent ciliary flush. The intraocular inflammation stimulates pupillary constriction.

MOTILITY

There are six extraocular muscles in each eye that are innervated by a total of three nerves. The action of a specific muscle can vary depending on the position of the eye when it is innervated. Table 1 shows the general relationships which apply.

Table 1 Extraocular muscle innervation		
Innervation	Muscle	Primary Action
3rd nerve	superior rectus	up
3rd nerve	medial rectus	in
3rd nerve	inferior rectus	down
3rd nerve	inferior oblique	up and in
4th nerve	superior oblique	down and in
6th nerve	lateral rectus	out

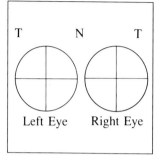
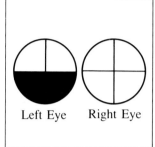
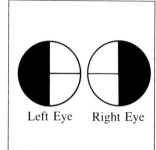

Fig. 4 (A) A normal gross visual field test. T=temporal
field; N=nasal field

Fig. 4 (B) An inferior field defect of the left eye; the right eye
is normal.

Fig. 4 (C) A complete bitemporal visual field defect.

The examiner should determine the range of ocular movements in all gaze posi-
tions (Fig. 1). Limited movement in any gaze position can be documented as –1 (min-
imal), –2 (moderate), –3 (severe), or –4 (total). For example, a patient with a complete
right sixth nerve palsy can be recorded as shown in Figure 2. Figure 3 shows a patient
with a blow-out fracture to the right orbit with entrapment of the inferior rectus muscle and limitation of upgaze.

CONFRONTATION VISUAL FIELDS

A visual field defect may be caused by a disturbance of any of the neurologic path-
ways for light transmission. This includes the retina, optic disc, optic nerve, optic chi-
asm, optic tract, optic radiations, or occipital cortex.

A screening test for gross visual field loss can be performed as follows:

1. One eye of the patient is covered.
2. With the uncovered eye the patient must maintain fixation, e.g., on the tip of the
   examiner's nose.
3. The examiner randomly projects fingers in any quadrant, while standing 3 or
   4 feet from the patient. For the detection of more subtle defects such as in optic
   neuritis, it is best to stand 10 to 20 feet away from the patient. The further one
   is from the patient, the greater the size of the scotoma.
4. The patient counts the projected fingers.

A normal response would be recorded as shown in Figure 4A. A patient with a retinal detachment of the superior retina would have an inferior field defect (Fig. 4B).
A patient with a pituitary tumor may present initially with visual loss and a complete
bitemporal defect (Fig. 4C). A more detailed evaluation of the visual field requires an
automated machine. The target size and luminosity can be varied and the patient's
response documented on a computer-generated printout.

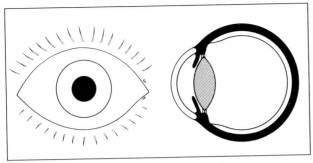 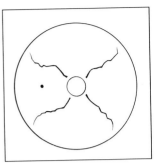

Fig. 5 Examination of the anterior segment includes an assessment of the lids, puncta, conjunctiva, sclera, cornea, anterior chamber, and lens.

Fig. 6 Examination of the posterior segment includes an assessment of the vessels, macula, and disc as well as the vitreous and peripheral retina.

ANTERIOR SEGMENT

Examination of the anterior segment should include an assessment of the lids, puncta, conjunctiva, sclera, cornea, anterior chamber, and lens (Fig. 5). In all suspected infectious cases, Q-tips are used or gloves are worn to depress or elevate lids. This protects the examiner from contamination.

Fluorescein stain can be used to detect deepithelialized surfaces, e.g., corneal abrasions, erosions, dendrites, and ulcers; epithelial defects stain green. Rose bengal stain also detects deepithelialized surfaces, and in addition stains devitalized cells, as are found in the conjunctiva in keratitis sicca or chemical toxicity.

When a superficial keratitis occurs without obvious evidence of a foreign body, the upper lid should be everted with the aid of a Q-tip to rule out the possibility of a lid margin or conjunctival foreign body.

POSTERIOR SEGMENT

Examination of the posterior segment should include an assessment of the vitreous, discs, vessels, maculae, and peripheral retina (Fig. 6).

Vitreous

The vitreous is a jellylike substance located between the lens and retina. With aging, the vitreous shrinks and often pulls away from its attachments to the retina and disc. Tissue or cells may be displaced, causing the symptom of vitreous floaters, or vitreous movements against the retina may result in the experience of flashing lights.

Vessels

The retinal blood vessels are normally transparent, and their color is due to the blood. During arteriosclerosis the blood vessel wall becomes visible, progressing from a "copper-wire" appearance to a later "silver-wire" color. Where arterioles meet

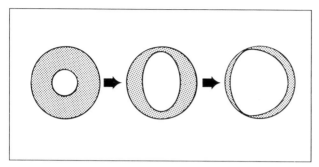

Fig. 7 Progressive cupping or increasing cup-to-disc ratio in the right eye in glaucoma

veins, a common sheath is found; thickening of the arteriole can cause indentation of the vein, or arteriovenous nicking. This can lead to thrombosis and vein occlusion.

Macula

The macula is the most light-sensitive area of the retina. In the center of the macula is a pit called the fovea which in young patients produces a well-defined reflex. If asymmetry in the foveal reflexes occurs in a patient with a visual disturbance, this suggests a retinal problem.

Optic Disc

The optic disc should be evaluated as follows:

1. *The Cup-to-Disc Ratio.* Most normal patients have a cup-to-disc (C/D) ratio of less than 0.5. A higher C/D ratio or asymmetry between the discs is suggestive of glaucoma. Figure 7 shows progressive cupping in glaucoma.

2. *Color of the Neural Rim.* A normal neural rim will have a pink color and should be similar in both eyes (Fig. 8A). In an old ischemic optic neuropathy the neural rim will be pale (Fig. 8B).

3. *Contour of the Disc Margins.* The disc margin contour should be distinct. In the acute stages of papilledema, optic neuritis, or ischemic optic neuropathy the disc may appear swollen and the margins indistinct (Fig. 9).

INTRAOCULAR PRESSURE

In an emergency case, the most important reason for checking intraocular pressure is to rule out acute angle closure glaucoma, in which condition the pressure is often greater than 40 mm Hg. A pressure over 22 mm Hg is generally considered above average and should prompt further investigation. The methods which can be used to check intraocular pressure include Schiotz tonometry, applanation tonometry, and air-puff tonometry.

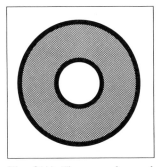 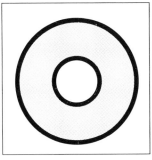 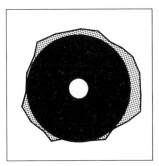

Fig. 8(A) The normal neural rim is pink

Fig. 8(B) The neural rim is pale in an old ischemic optic neuropathy.

Fig. 9 Hyperemia of the disc and indistinct disc margins may occur in papilledema, optic neuritis, or ischemic optic neuropathy.

Schiotz Tonometry

Schiotz tonometry is readily available in most emergency departments and doctors' offices, and is the technique of choice for the general practitioner. The patient is supine, a topical anesthetic is instilled in the eyes, the lids are separated, and then the tonometer is positioned on the central cornea. The reading on the scale is then converted to millimeters of mercury by a calibration chart.

Applanation Tonometry

The equipment for this test is not as readily available as the Schiotz tonometer. It is a slit lamp attachment that takes more experience to master, but results in a more accurate measurement.

Air-Puff Tonometer

The air-puff tonometer is an expensive instrument which is not readily available. It does not require use of a topical anesthetic, but is not as accurate as applanation tonometry.

Emergency Ocular Diseases

NONTRAUMATIC RED EYE (Appendix D)

Pre-Septal Cellulitis

Pre-septal cellulitis is characterized by erythema and swelling of the eyelids. The infection is confined to the anterior structures of the periorbita (Fig. 10).

Predisposing factors include a history of an upper respiratory tract infection, trauma to eyelids, or an external ocular infection. It must be differentiated from an orbital cellulitis, which can result in a permanent loss of vision. In a pre-septal cellulitis the patient has normal vision, no proptosis, normal ocular motility, and no pain with eye movements. *Hemophilus influenzae* is the organism most commonly associated with this condition in children under five years of age, and *Staphylococcus aureus* and *Streptococcus sp.* in adults.

Workup.
- Cultures are obtained from the nasopharynx, conjunctiva, and blood.
- The patient should be examined by an ophthalmologist to rule out orbital involvement.
- If the patient is unable to cooperate for the examination, or if there is any suspicion of orbital cellulitis, then a computed tomography (CT) scan should be ordered.

Treatment. In mild to moderate cases the prescribed therapy for pre-septal cellulitis is oral antibiotics:
- In adults, e.g., Keflex® 250 mg q.6h. for 10 days;
- In children, e.g., Ceclor® 40 mg/kg/day (maximum 1 gm/day) q.8h. for 10 days.
In severe cases intravenous antibiotics are administered. For example:
- In adults, nafcillin 1.5 and penicillin 3 million units q.4h.
- In children, ampicillin 200 mg/kg/day and chloramphenicol 11 mg/kg/day. If the organism proves sensitive to ampicillin, the chloramphenicol is discontinued.

Chalazion

Chalazion may be manifested initially as diffuse eyelid swelling which results from blockage of the duct of a meibomian gland (Fig. 11). Acutely, the obstruction may be secondary to infection by *Staphylococcus sp.* When the infection resolves, a painless nodule may remain which points to the skin or conjunctival side. Recurrent chalazia are often seen in association with blepharitis; appropriate treatment will decrease the incidence of this condition.

Workup. There is effectively no workup for the treatment of this condition.

Treatment
- Warm compresses can be applied for 10 minutes four times a day.

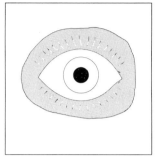 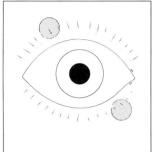 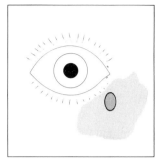

Fig. 10 Preseptal cellulitis is characterized by erythema and swelling of the eyelids.

Fig. 11 Chalazia are eyelid masses caused by obstruction of a meibomian gland.

Fig. 12 In acute dacryocystitis blockage of the lacrimal duct causes swelling and tenderness of the lacrimal sac.

- Topical antibiotic such as Bleph®-10 (sodium sulfacetamide) can be applied q.i.d.
- If the condition does not resolve in two to three weeks and is of cosmetic concern to the patient, the affected area can be incised and drained under local anesthesia; infants and children usually require general anesthesia. The incision is usually made on the conjunctival side of the tarsal plate, which obviates a skin incision and resultant scar.

Acute Dacryocystitis

Acute dacryocystitis is a blockage of the lacrimal duct which impedes the flow of tears through the lacrimal drainage system. Stasis occurs, which can result in a secondary bacterial infection and swelling and tenderness of the lacrimal sac (Fig. 12). The organism most commonly associated with this condition in children under five years of age is *Hemophilus influenzae*, and in adults is *Staphylococcus aureus* (usually penicillinase-resistant).

Workup. Pressure is applied to the lacrimal sac to express material through the puncta, and a conjunctival culture is prepared.

Treatment. In mild to moderate cases oral antibiotics are prescribed:
- In adults, Keflex 250 mg q.6h. for 10 days;
- In children, Ceclor 40 mg/kg (maximum 1 g/day) in divided doses every 8 hours for 10 days.

In severe cases intravenous antibiotics are administered as for pre-septal cellulitis:
- Adults may receive nafcillin 1.5 g and penicillin 3 million units q.4h.;
- Children may receive ampicillin 200 mg/kg/day and chloramphenicol 11 mg/kg/day. If the organism is sensitive to ampicillin, the chloramphenicol is discontinued.
- When the infection resolves, a dacryocystorhinostomy is recommended to provide a drainage channel for the tears.

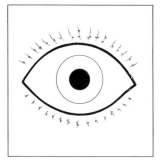 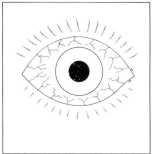 

Fig. 13 Blepharitis is characterized by debris on lashes, erythema of lid margins, and misdirection or loss of lashes.

Fig. 14 Allergic conjunctivitis is characterized by itching, redness, and chemosis.

Fig. 15 In adenoviral conjunctivitis the Keratitis may be absent or limited to superficial punctate keratitis and/or subepithelial infiltrates.

Blepharitis

Blepharitis is characterized by debris on the eyelashes, erythema of lid margins, and misdirection or loss of lashes (Fig. 13). It may be associated with conjunctivitis, keratitis, or neovascularization of the cornea. Blepharitis may be seborrheic, and/or secondary to *Staphylococcus sp.* Rarely, the lids may be infected by pediculosis.

Treatment of Staphylococcal and/or Seborrheic Blepharitis
- Warm compress should be applied b.i.d. to the eyelids to remove scales, and the lid margins cleansed with dilute Johnson's Baby Shampoo applied with a Q-tip.
- Erythromycin ointment may also be applied to the eyelids at bedtime.
- Artificial tears are used if there is associated keratitis or dry eye, e.g., Tears Plus®, or Liquifilm Tears® applied q.i.d.
- If these measures fail to resolve the problem, then the patient should be referred to an ophthamologist.
- A short course of a topical steroid/antibiotic combination such as Blephamide® may be useful, if there is significant inflammation.
- Tetracycline or doxicycline are useful in refractory cases.

Treatment of Pediculosis-associated Blepharitis. Pubic lice (pediculosis) involvement of the eyelids requires a distinct treatment:
- A 20% fluorescein solution applied to lashes will cause the adult lice to fall off.
- Eggs must be removed manually.
- A 30% incidence of other venereal diseases exists, and this should be ruled out by appropriate testing.

Allergic Conjunctivitis

Itching is the hallmark of allergic conjunctivitis. Other symptoms include tearing, redness, and chemosis (swelling of the conjunctiva), and the condition may be unilateral or bilateral (Fig. 14). The patient often has a history of allergies to dust, pollen, grass, cats, dogs, etc.

Workup
- Conjunctival scraping is optional.
- Giemsa stain may show eosinophils.

Treatment
- Cold compresses, topical antihistamine and vasoconstrictors (e.g., Albalon-A® q.i.d.) can be applied.
- If highly symptomatic, the patient should be referred to an ophthalmologist.
- A short course of a mild topical steroid (e.g., fluoromethodone (FML) q.i.d.) could be prescribed.

Adenoviral Conjunctivitis

Adenoviral conjunctivitis is a highly contagious disease (for up to 10 days) characterized by redness, tearing, and a variable degree of photophobia. Follicular hypertrophy of the conjunctiva, which is difficult to detect in the absence of a slit lamp, microscopically represents focal collections of lymphocytes. Keratitis may be absent or limited to superficial punctate keratitis or subepithelial infiltrates (Fig. 15). The enlarged preauricular lymph nodes are helpful in the diagnosis as they are never seen in bacterial conjunctivitis except with the gonococcal organism.

Workup. Cultures are unnecessary, since diagnosis is based on clinical evaluation.

Treatment
- No specific antiviral therapy is available.
- Cold compresses can be applied for patient comfort.
- Artificial tears (e.g., Tears Plus q.i.d.) or astringents (e.g., Albalon-A q.i.d.) can be used.
- Prophylactic precautions should be observed by the patient's family members and friends.
- Children should stay away from school for 7 to 10 days.
- If the examiner is uncertain of the diagnosis, it should be assumed that the cause is bacterial, and the condition treated with a topical antibiotic.

Bacterial Conjunctivitis

The symptoms of bacterial conjunctivitis are redness and purulent discharge (Fig. 16). There is no preauricular node enlargement except in cases of gonococcal conjunctivitis. This condition is less common than viral conjunctivitis.

Workup. In severe cases or those involving a neonate, a Gram stain and culture can be prepared.

Treatment
- Broad-spectrum antibiotics are prescribed, such as Sodium Sulamyd q.i.d.

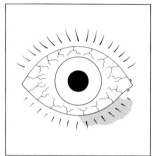

Fig. 16 Redness and purulent discharge are features of bacterial conjunctivitis.

Fig. 17 Chlamydial infection is characterized by redness, mucoid discharge, follicular hypertrophy, and superior micropannus as seen by slit lamp examination.

Fig. 18 Dendrite is the characteristic feature of herpes simplex keratitis.

- In children under five years of age infection may be by *Hemophilus influenzae*, and Choroptic® or Bleph-10 can be used as treatment.
- In cases of gonococcal conjunctivitis, the patient is admitted to hospital, and may be treated with intravenous antibiotics and topical application of bacitracin every half hour.

Chlamydia

This is a venereal disease which is usually seen in young sexually active adults. The ocular symptoms of chlamydial infection include redness and mucoid discharge, with or without photophobia. The preauricular lymph nodes may be enlarged (Fig. 17). Follicular hypertrophy of the conjunctiva is characteristically seen by slit lamp examination, and later in the disease course a superior micro-pannus of the cornea may develop. This condition is refractory to topical eye medications, and unlike adenoviral conjunctivitis which usually resolves in less than one month, it may become chronic if not treated.

Workup
- The patient should be referred to an ophthalmologist.
- Clinical diagnosis is made based on the signs and chronicity.
- A Giemsa stain, culture, and fluorescent antibody stain can be performed, but false negatives may occur.

Treatment. The standard treatment for this problem is oral:
- Tetracycline 250 mg q.i.d. for one month.
- The patient's sexual partner must be similarly treated for the same duration.

Herpes Simplex
Primary Herpes Simplex

The first exposure to herpes simplex virus in 90% of cases results in subclinical, usually mild disease. Resistance increases with age, so that primary infection is exceedingly rare in early adult life. Characteristically, the young child is infected by salivary contamination from an adult who has labial herpes. The incubation period is three to nine days. The clinical features of herpes simplex are both ocular and nonocular.

Ocular disease. Characteristics are vesicular eruption (especially lower lid and medial canthus), conjunctivitis, regional lymphadenopathy, and occasional corneal epithelial disease (Fig. 18). Symptoms are frequently unilateral.

Nonocular disease. The following forms of the disease may be present:
- Gingivostomatitis — The symptoms are fever, malaise, cervical lymphadenopathy, and sore throat.
- Pharyngitis — In college students, a primary attack of herpes simplex virus frequently results in a pharyngitis with vesicles on the tonsils.
- Cutaneous disease — Generally, type I occurs above the waist and type II below the waist. This disease may be seen in wrestlers, rugby players, and as a herpetic whitlow in dentists.
- Genital infection — Type II of the infection is more common than type I and is characterized by balanitis in males and cervicitis/vulvovaginitis in females. Patients may exhibit fever, myalgia, extensive vesicular lesions, and inguinaland pelvic lymphadenopathy.

Recurrent Herpes Simplex

The virus develops a "symbiosis" with man, and trigger mechanisms such as trauma, fever, sunlight, emotional stress, steroids, and menses provoke viral shedding, and immunological functions may be overcome. The trigeminal ganglion is a reservoir for the type I disease. The virus has a 50% recurrence rate over five years, and the recurring condition may be highly localized on the lips, nose, chin, eyes (lids, conjunctiva, corneal epithelium, corneal stroma, uvea), and genitals.

Workup. Since this is a clinical diagnosis, cultures are usually unnecessary.

Treatment. The various forms of herpes simplex require specific treatment:

- **Blepharitis** may occur without conjunctival or corneal disease. If it is recurrent, this is consistent with herpes simplex; herpes zoster does not recur. If there is skin but no lid involvement, no topical antiviral treatment is necessary. If the lid margin is involved, then prophylactic antivirals (e.g., Viroptic™ 5x/day) are applied to the conjunctiva.
- **Conjunctivitis** may occur without lid or corneal disease and the patient may

have an enlarged preauricular lymph ncde. Ophthalmic referral is recommended and an antiviral (e.g., Viroptic 9x/day) may be applied.

- **Keratitis** occurs in the following forms:
  - (i) **Punctate keratitis** is characterized by raised clusters of opaque epithelial cells, as evidenced with fluorescein stain. Referral to an ophthalmologist is recommended. If diagnosis is unequivocal, a topical antiviral (e.g., Viroptic 9x/day) may be applied. In the case of an equivocal diagnosis, treatment should be deferred and the patient followed closely.
  - (ii) **Dendritic keratitis** is recognized by desquamation in the center of plaques of swollen epithelial cells. The typical linear branching ulcer (stains with fluorescein) has overhanging margins of swollen opaque cells, which are laden with virus (stains with Rose-bengal). Ophthalmic referral is recommended and an antiviral (e.g., Viroptic 9x/day) should be applied.
  - (iii) **Geographic keratitis** results from progression of dendritic keratitis; a geographic epithelial defect (stain with fluorescein) is lined by heaped-up opaque cells (stain with Rose-bengal) and may be associated with steroid use in dendritic keratitis. Ophthalmic referral is recommended and an antiviral (e.g., Viroptic 9x/day) should be applied.
  - (iv) **Stromal keratitis** is an immunologic disease characterized by corneal stromal infiltrates and/or edema. Corneal inflammation that may be associated with iritis and keratic precipitates results from antibodies directed at viral antigens. Ophthalmic referral is recommended. If the epithelium is intact, a topical steroid, such as Pred Forte® 5x/day and an antiviral cover (e.g., Viroptic 5x/day) may be applied. If the stromal keratitis is associated with an epithelial disease, an antiviral (e.g., Viroptic 9x/day) should be applied until the epithelium heals (approximately 14 days), after which a topical steroid can be added.

Herpes Zoster

Herpes zoster tends to occur in children under 14 and in adults over 40 years of age. Its incidence is five times greater in those over 80 years of age than in adults between 20 and 40. A 50% incidence of AIDS has been found in male patients between the ages of 20 and 40 in New York City. The development of herpes zoster may be the first manifestation of AIDS.

The varicella virus which causes chickenpox can lie dormant in the sensory ganglia and later reactivate as shingles or herpes zoster. Causes of reactivation are unknown but may be related to aging, immune compromise (e.g., AIDS, lymphoproliferative diseases, systemic steroids), and trauma to the involved ganglion. Although chickenpox is contagious, it should not cause herpes zoster; however, children can develop chickenpox after contact with herpes zoster patients. Once the virus is reactivated, it may be contained (zoster sine herpete), or spread to the brain, skin, eye, or enter the bloodstream. The virus has a predilection for dermatome T3-L3, but the most common site is the trigeminal nerve. Cutaneous lesions of herpes zoster are histopatho-

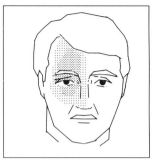

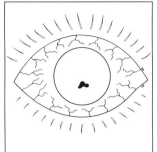

Fig. 19 Herpes zoster ophthalmicus is characterized by vesicular skin erruptions in the distribution of any of the branches of the trigeminal nerve.

Fig. 20 Recurrent corneal erosions stain with fluorescein.

Fig. 21 A ruptured vessel with blood accumulation in the subjunctival space is diagnosed as a subconjunctival hemorrhage.

logically identical to varicella, but have a greater inflammatory reaction which can cause scarring.

The dermatome pattern of herpes zoster may occur in three sites supplied by branches of the trigeminal nerve:

- The ophthalmic nerve distribution (V1) where it occurs 20 times more frequently than at the V2 or V3 sites. Frontal involvement is the most common, including the upper lid, forehead, and superior conjunctiva, which are supplied by supraorbital and supratrochlear branches (Fig. 19). Alternatively, it may spread to the lacrimal and nasociliary area which supplies the cornea, iris, ciliary body, and the tip of the nose;
- The maxillary nerve distribution (V2);
- The mandibular nerve distribution (V3).

The virus may affect none, any, or all of these branches. Involvement of the nasociliary nerve often leads to infection of the eye. Hutchinson's rule (1860s) states that ocular involvement is frequent, if the side of the tip of the nose is involved.

Clinically, herpes zoster is characterized by a prodrome, skin disease, and ocular complications. The patients may experience pain, burning, itching, hyperesthesia in the dermatome area, followed by erythema, macules, papules, and vesicles which become confluent and may form deeply pitted scars (dermis affected by necrotic process). Ocular complications include lid scarring and exposure, muscle palsies, conjunctivitis, episcleritis, scleritis, keratitis, uveitis, and retinitis.

Workup. Systemic evaluation for underlying malignancy is not indicated since the yield is low.

Treatment.
- Compresses can be applied to the affected areas of the skin.
- Medication for pain relief can be given.

- Antivirals may be prescribed: acyclovir 600 mg P.O. 5x/day for 10 days may prevent serious ocular disease and may accelerate resolution of skin lesions. It is more effective if it is started within 72 hours of the onset of the disease and it has no effect on preventing postherpetic neuralgia. Topical antiviral therapy is ineffective treatment for the eye.
- Systemic steroids (e.g., prednisone) for two to three weeks may be prescribed for patients over 60 years of age, since this is the age group most susceptible to postherpetic neuralgia. However, steroids may cause disseminated herpes zoster, and therefore should not be given in immunodeficient patients.
- The patient should be referred to an ophthalmologist to rule out ocular involvement.
- Topical steroids (e.g., Pred Forte q.i.d.) will improve comfort and decrease the chance of corneal scarring.
- Cycloplegic agents (e.g., Cyclogyl 2% b.i.d.) will relieve ciliary spasm in corneal and anterior chamber inflammation making the patient more comfortable and dilating the pupil to prevent posterior synechiae (iris-lens adhesions).

Recurrent Corneal Erosions

Patients with recurrent corneal erosions experience pain, photophobia, and redness, but have no acute history of trauma. Corneal erosion, which stains with fluorescein (Fig. 20), is due to the lack of strong corneal epithelial attachments. The erosion frequently occurs on awakening, since the corneal epithelium becomes more edematous during eyelid closure and more susceptible to focal sloughing. Predisposing factors for this condition may be an old traumatic injury (e.g., fingernail, tree branch, paper), corneal dystrophy, and bullous keratopathy (i.e., corneal edema).

Workup. No workup is required.

Treatment
- Antibiotic ointment or drops (e.g., Sodium Sulamyd) and a cycloplegic agent (e.g., Cyclogyl 1%) should be prescribed.
- A pressure patch should be applied.
- Ophthalmic referral is recommended.
- Hypertonic drops and/or ointment, e.g., sodium chloride 5% drops during the day and ointment at bedtime to be used over a period of weeks to months to dehydrate the epithelium and decrease the risk of erosions.
- Anterior stromal puncture can be performed if the patient continues to develop erosions in the same location. A 25-gauge needle can be used to make multiple punctures into the anterior stroma in the area of the erosion. This allows for the development of stronger adhesions and decreases the risk of erosions. However, the technique is contraindicated in erosions that occur close to the pupillary axis.

Subconjunctival Hemorrhage

A ruptured vessel with blood accumulation in the subconjunctival space describes a subjunctival hemorrhage (Fig. 21). It is often accompanied by a history of coughing,

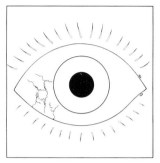 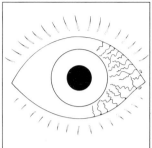 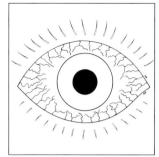

Fig. 22 Phylectenules are small, pinkish-white nodules surrounded by conjunctival hyperemia which occur most frequently near the limbus.

Fig. 23 Sectoral episcleritis is characterized by a salmon-pink color of the conjunctival and episcleral tissues.

Fig. 24 A purplish hue and injection of conjunctival and deep episcleral vessels are signs of scleritis.

vomiting or straining. The patient may be taking coumadin or aspirin.

Workup
- If the patient's history is negative for Valsalva maneuvers, a blood pressure reading should be taken.
- The patient on coumadin should undergo tests to ensure that the rate of blood clotting is in the desired range.
- In the case of recurrent subconjunctival hemorrhage, a complete blood count should be taken to rule out a blood dyscrasia.

Treatment. Reassuring the patient is all that is necessary since the hemorrhage will resolve spontaneously.

Phylectenule

A phylectenule is a small pinkish-white nodule in the center of a hyperemic area of conjunctiva (Fig. 22). Although it is seen most frequently near the limbus, it may occur anywhere on the bulbar conjunctiva. Less commonly, it involves the cornea where it is associated with vascular ingrowth. The patient's history should be used to rule out the possiblity of any foreign body. Phylectenules may be caused by a hypersensitivity reaction to an antigenic stimulus such as *Staphylococcus aureus* or the tubercle bacilli.

Workup
- The patient should be referred to an ophthalmologist.
- A tuberculin skin test and chest X ray are recommended if the patient is in a high-risk group.

Treatment.
- A topical steroid (e.g., Pred Forte q.i.d.) may be prescribed.
- Any associated staphylococcal blepharitis should be treated.

Episcleritis
Episcleritis is characterized by a salmon-pink hue of the superficial layer of the eye, with involvement of the conjunctiva and episclera (Fig. 23). At least one-third of the lesions are tender to touch. Simple episcleritis may be sectorial in 70% or generalized in 30% of the patients. In nodular episcleritis, unlike in nodular scleritis, the nodules which form are moveable with a Q-tip.

Workup. Ophthalmic referral is recommended.

Treatment. A topical steroid (e.g., FML or Pred Forte q.i.d.) will cause resolution of the inflammation.

Scleritis
Scleritis is frequently bilateral and, characteristically, associated with pain. The ocular surface has a purplish hue with involvement of the deep episcleral vessels (Fig. 24). Systemic diseases, such as collagen vascular, ulcerative colitis, Crohn's disease, and sarcoidosis, are present in 50% of patients. The eight-year mortality rate is 30%, with death usually due to a vascular disease. Scleritis may be classified as simple (in its most benign form), nodular (the nodule is immobile when pushed with a Q-tip), or necrotizing (the majority of these patients have rheumatoid arthritis).

Workup
- Ophthalmic referral is recommended.
- The patient should be evaluated for an underlying systemic disease.

Treatment
- A topical steroid (e.g., Pred Forte) may be prescribed to reduce the inflammation.
- A systemic nonsteroidal anti-inflammatory medication is recommended (e.g., Indocid® 25 mg P.O. t.i.d.).

Corneal Ulcers
Patients with corneal ulcers may experience redness, pain, photophobia, and tearing. The cornea will have a whitish infiltrate with an overlying epithelial defect that will stain with fluorescein (Fig. 25). Patients most at risk are those who wear contact lenses, those with blepharitis and dry eyes, or those who have experienced corneal trauma. The most common causes are bacterial infections, e.g., by *Pseudomonas*, *Staphylococcus aureus*, or *Streptococcus pneumoniae*.

Workup
- Ophthalmic referral is recommended.

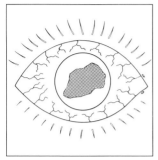
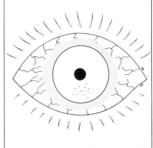

Fig. 25 Corneal ulcers—The epithelial defect which overlies the whitish corneal infiltrate stains with fluorescein.

Fig. 26 In iritis ciliary flush is prominent, the pupil is constricted, and slit lamp examination reveals keratic precipitates.

- The cornea should be scraped for Gram's stain and culture.

Treatment. Topical fortified antibiotics, e.g. tobramycin (15 mg/mL) and cefazolin (50 mg/mL) can be applied.

Iritis

Iritis is characterized by redness, photophobia, tearing, and decreased vision. A ciliary flush is prominent and the pupil is constricted secondary to the inflammation (Fig. 26). Slit lamp examination shows an anterior chamber reaction manifested by inflammatory cells and flare (protein leakage), and keratic precipitates. Testing with fluorescein stain should be done to rule out a corneal abrasion and herpes simplex dendrite.

Workup
- Ophthalmic referral is recommended.
- If condition is persistent or recurrent, underlying systemic disorders (e.g., ankylosing spondylitis, sarcoidosis) should be ruled out.

Treatment. A topical steroid (e.g., Pred Forte q.1-2h.) and a cycloplegic agent (e.g., Cyclogyl 1% or homatropine 5% q.6h.) should be prescribed.

Acute Angle Closure Glaucoma

Acute angle closure glaucoma is characterized by redness, severe pain, photophobia, and decreased vision (Fig. 27); the patient may also experience nausea and vomiting. Elevated intraocular pressure, corneal edema, and a nonreactive mid-dilated pupil may also be present. This tends to occur more frequently in the hyperopic (farsighted) eye due to a relatively narrow anterior chamber.

Workup
- Tonometry should be performed to confirm diagnosis.

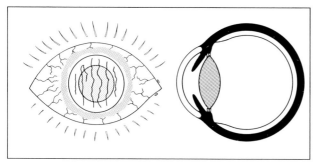

Fig. 27 Acute angle closure glaucoma is manifested by elevated intraocular pressure, associated with redness, ciliary injection, corneal edema, a nonreactive mid-dilated pupil, and a relatively narrow anterior chamber angle.

- Ophthalmic referral is recommended.

Treatment
- Effective medications include: pilocarpine 2% q.5min. x4 then q.1.h., Betagan™ drops q.12h., isosorbide 1-2 gm/kg P.O. x1, Diamox® 250 mg P.O. q.6h. or 500 mg I.V. mannitol 20% 1-2 gm/kg IV.
- Laser iridotomy can be performed in the affected eye and a prophylactic iridotomy in the contralateral eye.

TRAUMATIC RED EYE

Corneal Abrasions
The patient with a corneal abrasion has a history of trauma caused, for example, by a tree branch, fingernail, or contact lens. The patient will complain of pain, photophobia, redness, and blurred vision.

Workup. The diagnosis is confirmed by demonstrating an epithelial defect with fluorescein dye (Fig. 28).

Treatment
- Antibiotic drop or ointment (e.g., Bleph-10) should be instilled along with a cycloplegic agent (e.g., Cyclogyl 1% or homatropine 5%).
- A pressure patch should be applied.
- Analgesic medication may make the patient more comfortable.
- Patient follow-up is recommended on a daily basis to determine epithelial healing and ensure the absence of an infection.

N.B.: Contact lens related abrasions should not be patched, as a subclinical infection may be present. Instead, these abrasions should be treated with antibiotic drops active against *Pseudomonas* (e.g., tobramycin q.2h.).

Fig. 28 Corneal abrasion is characterized by an epithelial defect (which stains with fluorescein) and ciliary injection.

Fig. 29 Ultraviolet keratitis is characterized by a superficial punctate keratitis which stains with fluorescein associated with ciliary injection and blepharospasm.

Fig. 30 Depending on the type and severity, signs of chemical injury may include conjunctivitis, superficial punctate keratitis, epithelial defects of the cornea and conjunctiva, blanching of blood vessels, and necrosis of tissues.

Contact Lens

Contact lens wearers may develop a red eye due to a variety of pathophysiologic causes: mechanical, hypoxic, immunologic, chemical toxicity, and infection. The most important concern is the possibility of the development of an infected ulcer that can lead to corneal scarring and a permanent decrease in vision.

Workup. Refer to Appendix E for the differential diagnosis of red eye in contact lens wearers.

Treatment
- All patients with a red eye should remove their contact lenses.
- Referral to an ophthalmologist is necessary to determine the cause of red eye.

Ultraviolet Keratitis

Ultraviolet keratitis is usually bilateral and is characterized by redness, photophobia, tearing, and blepharospasm (Fig. 29). Usually the patient has been welding or using a sunlamp without proper eye protection. Typically, the symptoms appear 6 to 10 hours after exposure.

Workup. Fluorescein staining will reveal the presence of superficial punctate keratitis.

Treatment
- An antibiotic drop or ointment (e.g., Bleph-10) should be instilled along with a cycloplegic agent (e.g., Cyclogyl 1%).
- The more severely affected eye should be patched, and the patient instructed to apply a patch to the less affected eye at home.

- A pain medication can be prescribed.
- Follow-up is recommended to ensure epithelial healing.

Chemical Injuries

Alkali injuries are often more severe than acid injuries due to the fact that acids tend to coagulate tissue and inhibit further penetration into the cornea. Clinical findings of chemical injury vary with severity of the injury: a mild injury is characterized by conjunctivitis, superficial punctate keratitis, and an epithelial defect of the cornea and conjunctiva; a severe injury exhibits blanching of limbal blood vessels and opacification of the cornea (Fig. 30).

Alkali Agents
- Ammonia — Commonly found in household ammonia (7% cleaning agent), fertilizer, and refrigerant (strongest concentration is 29%). Penetration of the eye occurs in less than a minute, which makes the injury difficult to treat by irrigation.
- Lye (sodium hydroxide) — Commonly found in drain cleaners (e.g., Draino), it ranks second to ammonia in severity of injury induced.
- Hydroxides — Common forms are potassium hydroxide (found in caustic potash) and magnesium hydroxide (found in sparklers and flares). The chemical burns are similar to those caused by sodium hydroxide.
- Lime ($CaOH_2$=calcium hydroxide) — This is one of the most common substances involved in ocular burns and is found in plaster, cement, mortar, and whitewash. However, because it reacts with the epithelial cell membrane to form calcium soaps which precipitate, it penetrates the eye poorly.

Acid Agents
- Sulfuric Acid (H_2SO_4) — Commonly found in batteries and industrial chemicals, injuries are often due to battery explosions with resultant lacerations, contusions, and foreign bodies. When H_2SO_4 comes into contact with the water in the corneal tissue, heat is released charring the tissue and causing severe injury.
- Sulfur Dioxide (SO_2) — Commonly found combined with oils in fruit and vegetable preservatives, bleach, and refrigerant. It forms sulfurous acid (H_2SO_3) when it combines with water in corneal tissue. Injury is caused by the H_2SO_3 rather than the freezing effect of SO_2; it denatures proteins, inactivates numerous enzymes, and penetrates tissue well because of its high lipid – and water-solubility.
- Hydrofluoric Acid (HF) — Commonly used for etching and polishing glass or silicone, frosted glass, refined uranium and beryllium, alkylation of high octane gasoline, production of elemental fluoride, inorganic fluorides, and organic fluorocarbons. Much of the damage to the eye is caused by the fluoride ion.
- Other Acids — These include chromic acid, hydrochloric acid, nitric acid and acetic acid.

Workup. Since this emergency situation requires immediate treatment, no workup is recommended.

Treatment. The emergency physician should initiate the following procedures:
- The eye should be irrigated with a nontoxic liquid (water, ionic solutions, buffered solutions), but acidic solutions are not recommended as they are too risky. An I.V. drip for at least 30 minutes is recommended with the eyelids retracted. The pH can be checked using litmus paper, although this is optional.
- Any particulate matter should be removed from the fornices. A moistened cotton-tip applicator can be used to remove chemical matter.
- A cycloplegic agent (e.g., Cyclogyl or homatropine) will prevent posterior synechiae and alleviates ciliary spasm.
- An antibiotic ointment can be applied, along with a pressure patch.

The ophthalmologist may initiate the following treatment:
- The patient should be followed closely to ensure the healing of the epithelium.
- The intraocular pressure should be lowered, if it is elevated (e.g., prescribe Betagan and/or Diamox).
- Topical steroids may be used to decrease inflammation but should be limited to no more than two weeks in the case of a persistent epithelial defect. Prolonged steroid use in the presence of an epithelial defect can cause the cornea to melt.
- Bandage contact lenses may be used, if the epithelium is not healed by patching.
- If the cornea heals with scarring and vascularization, the prognosis for restoring vision using a corneal transplant is poor because of the high incidence of graft rejection and failure.

Corneal Foreign Bodies

A corneal foreign body may be present in the patient exhibiting redness, foreign-body sensation, photophobia, and a history of trauma (Fig. 31).

Workup. None is required.

Treatment.
- A topical anesthetic should be instilled and the foreign body removed with a needle (e.g., 22-gauge) or a burr drill. If the foreign body cannot be seen, the upper lid should be everted to examine the lid margin and the palpebral conjunctival surface.
- A cycloplegic agent (e.g., Cyclogyl 1%) should be instilled, along with an antibiotic drop or ointment (e.g., Bleph-10).
- A pressure patch should be applied.
- Follow-up is recommended to determine epithelial healing, and to ensure the absence of infection or residual rust.

Intraocular Foreign Bodies

A small, foreign body traveling at a high speed can penetrate the eye without the patient's awareness. The symptoms are highly variable, depending on the site of penetration and intraocular structures affected. All foreign bodies made of iron should be removed, since they can cause significant intraocular damage (siderosis bulbi). However, glass, aluminum, gold, and silver are inert and usually cause little or no chronic intraocular damage (Fig. 32).

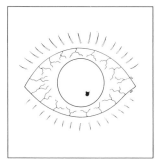 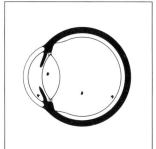

Fig. 31 Redness, foreign-body sensation, and photophobia occur in the presence of a corneal foreign body.

Fig. 32 Intraocular foreign bodies can be found in a variety of sites: in the anterior chamber, lens, vitreous, or retina.

Workup
- An X ray (Waters' view and lateral) should be ordered if an intraocular foreign body is suspected.
- Ophthalmic referral is recommended.
- If the foreign body cannot be visualized on examination, a CT scan should be ordered to determine whether the foreign body is intraocular or extraocular.

Treatment. To extract an intraocular foreign body, magnetic extraction or vitrectomy with foreign body instrumentation is usually indicated. Most foreign bodies outside of the eye in the orbit can usually be left without adverse sequelae.

Blow-Out Fracture

A blow to the periorbital structures can cause a fracture of the orbital floor and result in periorbital ecchymosis, infraorbital nerve anesthesia, and limitation of upgaze. There are two theories as to the mechanism of a blow-out fracture: (1) That a blow to the orbit causes a sudden increase in intraorbital pressure which results in the fracture; (2) A blow to the inferior orbital rim results in a buckling of the orbital floor.

Workup
- An X ray (Waters' view and lateral) and a CT scan (anteroposterior and coronal views of orbits) should be taken.
- Ophthalmic referral is recommended.
- The eye should be checked for any associated intraocular damage (e.g., hyphema, scleral rupture, traumatic cataract, macular edema, choroidal rupture, retinal tears, or retinal detachment).

Treatment
- Patients should try to refrain from nose-blowing and coughing.
- Systemic antibiotics should be prescribed (e.g., Keflex 250 mg P.O. q.i.d. x 10 days).

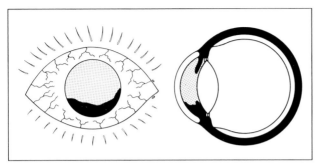

Fig. 33 Usually the result of blunt trauma, hyphema (or blood in the anterior chamber) is characterized by decreased vision, ciliary injection, and a hazy view of the fundus due to the presence of blood.

- Surgical repair of the orbital fracture is dependent on the CT scan findings and/or clinical signs during the subsequent one to two weeks.
- Surgery is indicated in cases of soft tissue entrapment associated with diplopia, enophthalmos greater than 2 mm, and fractures involving more than one-half of the orbital floor.

Hyphema

Hyphema is usually caused by trauma from a blunt object and is characterized by decreased vision, ciliary injection, and a view of the fundus which is hazy due to the presence of blood (Fig. 33). Children often have an unreliable history, and it is important to rule out any intraocular foreign body. A tear in the ciliary body or iris usually occurs in the area of the angle. The incidence of rebleeds is 20 to 25%, usually between the third and fifth day.

Workup. No workup is recommended.

Treatment
- Ophthalmic referral is recommended.
- A protective eye shield should be applied.
- Hospital admittance should include bedrest with bathroom privileges.
- A cycloplegic agent and antiglaucoma medication should be prescribed.
- Amicar® (aminocaproic acid) reduces the incidence of secondary hemorrhage and may be taken orally by the patient.
- Patients should be told that they are at an increased risk for the development of glaucoma secondary to damage to the angle, as well as for retinal detachment. Patients therefore should be followed on a regular basis for the rest of their lives.

Blunt Trauma Injury

Hyphema, cataract, iridodialysis, scleral rupture, traumatic mydriasis, choroidal rupture, retinal tears and/or retinal detachment may be present in blunt trauma injuries.

Workup. No workup is required.

Treatment
- Ophthalmic referral is recommended.
- A protective eye shield should be applied.
- Cataracts, scleral ruptures, retinal tears, and/or retinal detachments should be surgically managed.
- Any associated hyphema should be treated as previously described.

Lacerations

Workup. No workup is required.

Treatment
- Ophthalmic referral is recommended.
- A protective eye shield should be applied.

The following are the treatment options depending on the affected sites:
- (i) Lid — if the lid margin is involved, a suturing technique is critical to prevent notching.
- (ii) Conjunctiva — if an isolated injury, repair is usually unnecessary.
- (iii) Sclera — always suspect a puncture or laceration when the conjunctiva is involved; scleral laceration requires sutures and treatment with I.V. antibiotics to prevent endophthalmitis.
- (iv) Cornea — full-thickness lacerations require sutures, and puncture wounds that leak can be glued with tissue adhesives.
- (v) Lens — cataract extraction is indicated for this injury.
- (vi) Vitreous — a vitrectomy should be performed.

DECREASED VISION IN WHITE EYE

The emergency physician should be able to make the diagnosis of a sudden decrease in vision. Early treatment of central retinal artery occlusion and ischemic neuropathy secondary to giant cell arteritis can be sight-saving.

Vein Occlusion

The presence of scattered superficial retinal hemorrhages may indicate a central retinal vein occlusion (CRVO) or a branch retinal vein occlusion (BRVO) (Fig. 34). In CRVO the hemorrhages are located primarily at the posterior pole but may be seen throughout the fundus; in BRVO the hemorrhages are located in the distribution of the occluded vein.

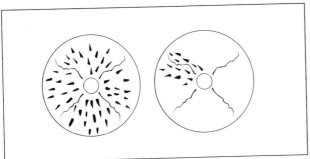

Fig. 34 Scattered superficial retinal hemorrhages are indicative of *left*: central retinal vein occlusion or *right*: branch retinal vein occlusion.

Workup
- Ophthalmic referral is recommended.
- The intraocular pressure in both eyes should be taken, since patients with vein occlusions have a higher incidence of glaucoma.
- Fluorescein angiography may be performed to determine the extent of retinal ischemia and/or macular edema.

Treatment
- In CRVO, pan-retinal laser photocoagulation is indicated, if the retina shows significant ischemic change. This technique prevents the neovascularization of the anterior chamber angle which can lead to glaucoma.
- In BRVO, focal laser photocoagulation may improve visual acuity and may be indicated for chronic macular edema. If neovascularization of the retina develops, then focal laser photocoagulation may resolve the neovascular tufts and prevent a vitreous hemorrhage.

Artery Occlusion
Both central retinal artery occlusions (CRAO) and branch retinal artery occulusions (BRAO) are characterized by ischemic whitening of the retina. In CRAO the fovea appears as a cherry-red spot, since the choroidal vasculature is easily visible through this relatively thinned retinal area (Fig. 35). Central visual acuity may rarely be normal in CRAO, if the blood supply from the choroidal vasculature to the fovea is maintained by a small retinal artery (cilioretinal artery). Most occlusions are caused by emboli that may be seen on the disc in CRAO or in an artery in BRAO.

Workup
- The patient's history should be taken to determine whether cerebral transient ischemic attacks have occurred.
- The carotid arteries and the heart should be evaluated to determine the source of the emboli.

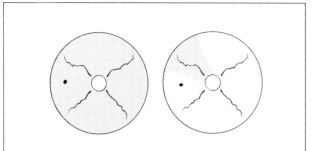

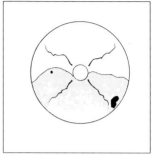

Fig. 35 Ischemic whitening of the retina is indicative of *left*: a central retinal artery occlusion or *right*: a branch retinal artery occlusion.

Fig. 36 In retinal detachment the retina appears white when elevated. If the macula is detached, the central vision will be diminished.

Treatment
- Less than four hours by history is a true emergency.
- The patient should be given an ocular massage, along with Betagan drops, Diamox 500 mg P.O., and mannitol 20% 200 mL I.V.
- Ophthalmic referral is recommended.

Retinal Detachment

When a retinal tear develops, fluid may accumulate beneath the retina creating a retinal detachment. A visual field deficit is present and the retina appears white when elevated (Fig. 36). There is an increased risk of retinal detachment in patients with myopia, aphakia, pseudophakia, or previous ocular trauma.

Workup. No workup is required.

Treatment
- Ophthalmic referral is recommended.
- Surgical correction is required.
- If the patient's vision is diminished (i.e., the macula is detached), there appears to be no difference in final visual acuity whether the surgery is performed immediately or after two or three days.

Maculopathy

A sudden decrease in vision often associated with metamorphosia (wavy vision) suggests a macular problem. The macula may be affected by edema, hemorrhage, and/or exudates. Differential diagnosis includes diabetes mellitus, macular degeneration, histoplasmosis, and central serous retinopathy.

Workup
- Ophthalmic referral is recommended.
- Fluorescein angiography may be performed to determine the source of macular leakage.

Treatment
- If leaking vessels and/or microaneurysms are identified in diabetic patients, laser photocoagulation can be performed.
- In the case of choroidal neovascularization in macular degeneration or histoplasmosis, laser photocoagulation can be applied if the vessels are not directly beneath the fovea.
- In central serous retinopathy, a fluorescein angiogram will often identify a focal leakage point of the retinal pigment epithelium which causes an accumulation of fluid beneath the retina. The majority of cases resolve spontaneously. However, the course can be shortened by using a laser to seal the defect in the pigment epithelium.

Vitreous Hemorrhage

Vitreous hemorrhage is characterized by a hazy view of the fundus. The most common causes are posterior vitreous detachment, proliferative diabetic retinopathy, vein occlusion with neovascularization of the retina, retinal tear without detachment, retinal detachment, macroaneurysm of the retina, and trauma.

Workup
- Ophthalmic referral is recommended.
- A B-scan ultrasound should be taken to rule out associated retinal detachment and/or mass lesions such as a malignant melanoma.

Treatment
- The majority of hemorrhages will resolve spontaneously in a few weeks to months.
- Vitrectomy may be indicated in nonclearing vitreous hemorrhages. It may also be combined with laser photocoagulation if there is an associated retinal tear or neovascularization, or a scleral buckle if there is a retinal detachment.

Optic Neuritis

Optic neuritis is usually seen in patients between 20 and 50 years of age, who complain of a decrease in vision and pain with eye movement. Patients usually have decreased color vision. The optic disc is swollen or it may appear normal in retrobulbar optic neuritis (Fig. 37). Of these patients, 40% will develop multiple sclerosis.

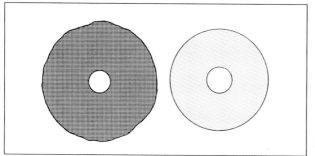 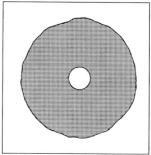

Fig. 37 Optic neuritis is characterized by *(left:)* a swollen optic disc and indistinct disc margins; or *(right)* a normal appearing disc in retrobulbar optic neuritis.

Fig. 38 Ischemic optic neuropathy is accompanied by a pale swelling of the optic disc and indistinct disc margins.

Workup
- Ophthalmic referral is recommended.
- The visual field should be checked and a follow-up test performed to determine the course of visual loss.
- If the initial visual field is atypical or if vision does not improve over six weeks, a CT scan should be taken to rule out a compressive lesion.

Treatment
- No specific ocular therapy is generally indicated.
- Controlled studies of systemic steriods have failed to demonstrate any difference in long-term outcome between treated and untreated groups. However, steroids have been shown to shorten the duration of the acute attack in some patients. Therefore, patients with visual loss in both eyes may benefit from steroidal therapy, e.g., prednisone 80 mg/day tapered over 2 to 3 weeks.

Ischemic Optic Neuropathy

Ischemic optic neuropathy is usually seen in patients over 50 years of age and is characterized by a sudden decrease in vision and a swollen optic disc (Fig. 38). The disease process is idiopathic in the majority of cases. Occasionally the condition is secondary to giant cell arteritis (GCA). This is an inflammatory condition of medium to large arteries with a predilection for extradural cranial arteries including the ophthalmic vessels. The symptoms and signs of GCA are headache, jaw claudication, and temporal artery tenderness, but it is important to note that patients with GCA may exhibit only visual symptoms.

Workup
- The erythrocyte sedimentation rate (ESR) should be obtained to rule out GCA. In this condition the ESR is usually elevated.
- Temporal artery biopsy is the definitive test to confirm the diagnosis.

Treatment
- No specific treatment exists for idiopathic ischemic optic neuropathy.
- Ophthalmic referral is recommended.
- If GCA is present, systemic steroids should be started immediately to protect the patient from bilateral visual loss.
- Steroids are usually tapered and maintained for a minimum of 9 to 12 months.

DIPLOPIA

Third Nerve Palsy
The third nerve innervates four eye muscles: the superior rectus, the medial rectus, the inferior rectus, and the inferior oblique. It carries the parasympathetic fibers to the sphincter of the iris, and innervates the levator muscle of the upper lid.

In third nerve palsy there may be diplopia, ptosis, and/or a dilated pupil. The eye is deviated out and down. The etiology of this condition is as follows: aneurysm 20%, vascular disease (diabetes, hypertension, atherosclerosis) 20%, tumors 15%, trauma 15%, and miscellaneous and undetermined 30%.

Workup
- If the pupil is fixed and dilated, other causes should be ruled out (e.g., Adie's pupil, or contamination with a dilating drop).
- If the pupillary dilatation is secondary to third nerve palsy, this constitutes a medical emergency and neurosurgical referral is required. Cerebral angiography and CT scan should be ordered to rule out intracranial aneurysm or neoplasm. If the pupil is not involved, diabetes, hypertension, collagen vascular disease, and giant cell arteritis (if the patient is more than 55 years of age) should be ruled out.

Treatment
- Ophthalmic referral is recommended.
- The eye can be patched to alleviate diplopia.
- The majority of third nerve palsies not involving the pupil resolve within six months.
- If muscle weakness persists for more than 12 months, then surgery can be performed to improve cosmesis.

Fourth Nerve Palsy

The fourth nerve supplies the superior oblique muscle which moves the eye downward and inward. The palsy causes elevation of the eye with resultant vertical diplopia and involves a torsional component making images appear tilted. Congenital fourth nerve palsies may initially be asymptomatic and a head tilt may be the only symptom; as image fusion ability diminishes over time, diplopia results. Acquired fourth nerve palsies are usually secondary to head trauma.

Workup
- If the fourth nerve palsy is isolated, it is not necessary to test for any underlying systemic diseases.

Treatment
- Ophthalmic referral is recommended.
- Prismatic correction in eyeglasses or surgical intervention may be indicated, depending on the severity and the duration of the palsy.

Sixth Nerve Palsy

The sixth nerve innervates the lateral rectus muscle which moves the eye out. A palsy is characterized by horizontal diplopia (images side-by-side), most prominent in the field of gaze of the underactive lateral rectus muscle. The patient may be partially or completely unable to move the eye laterally.

Workup
- Obtain a patient history; children often have a history of a recent viral illness or immunization.
- In adults, diabetes, hypertension, collagen vascular disease, and GCA (if over the age of 55) should be ruled out.
- If sixth nerve palsy is not isolated (i.e., associated with other nerve palsies) or if the patient has papilledema, then a CT scan is indicated to rule out a neoplastic process.

Treatment
- Ophthalmic referral is recommended.
- Isolated sixth nerve palsies usually resolve spontaneously within six months.
- An eye patch can be placed over the affected eye, or if the patient wears eyeglasses, tape can be placed over the lateral portion of the lens.
- If muscle weakness persists for more than 12 months, then surgery can align the eyes in primary gaze.

Appendixes

Appendix A
Ocular complications of systemic diseases

Disease	Possible Ocular Findings
Diabetes mellitus	• Background retinopathy: retinal hemorrhages, exudates & microaneurysms. • Preproliferative retinopathy: cotton-wool spots, intraretinal microvascular abnormalities. • Proliferative retinopathy: neovascularization, preretinal hemorrhage, vitreous hemorrhage, retinal detachment.
Graves' disease	Lid retraction, exposure keratopathy, chemosis and injection, restriction of eye movements, proptosis, compressive optic neuropathy.
Hypertension	Sclerosis of vessels in longstanding disease; narrowing of vessels, retinal hemorrhages, and/or exudates in severe hypertension.
Rheumatoid arthritis & other collagen vascular diseases	Dry eye, episcleritis, scleritis, peripheral corneal ulceration and/or melting.
Cancer	Metastatic disease to choroid may result in retinal detachment; disease in the orbit can result in proptosis and restriction of eye movements (e.g., breast, lung cancer).

| **Appendix B** | |
| Lifesaving ocular signs | |
Findings	Clinical Significance
White pupil	In an infant retinoblastoma must be ruled out.
Aniridia (iris appears absent)	May be autosomal dominant (2/3s) or sporadic inheritance. In sporadic cases where the short arm of chromosome 11 is deleted, there is a 90% risk of developing Wilm's tumor; the risk in other sporadic cases is approximately 20%.
Thickened corneal nerves (slit lamp)	Part of the multiple endocrine neoplasia syndrome type IIB. Must rule out medullary carcinoma of the thyroid, pheochromocytoma, and parathyroid adenomas.
Retinal angioma	May be part of the Von Hippel-Lindau syndrome. Autosomal dominant inheritance with variable penetrance. Must rule out hemangioblastomas of the central nervous system, renal cell carcinoma, and pheochromocytoma.
Multiple pigmented patches of fundus	Lesions represent patches of congenital hypertrophy of the retinal pigment epithelium. May be part of Gardner's syndrome characterized by multiple premalignant intestinal polyps together with benign soft tissue tumors (lipomas, fibromas, sebaceous cysts) and osteomas of the skull and jaw. A complete gastrointestinal investigation is indicated. If a diagnosis of Gardner's syndrome is made, prophylactic colectomy is indicated because of the potential for malignant degeneration of colonic polyps.
Third nerve palsy with a dilated pupil	Must rule out an intracranical aneurysm or neoplastic lesion. CT scan should be performed on an emergency basis.
Papilledema	Must rule out an intracranial mass lesion. CT scan should be performed on an emergency basis.
Pigmentary degeneration of the retina and motility disturbance	May represent the Kearns-Sayre syndrome. Must rule out a cardiac conduction defect disturbance with an annual electrocardiogram. May develop an intraventricular conduction defect, bundle block, bifascicular disease, or complete heart block. Patient must be prepared for the possible need to implant a pacemaker.

Appendix C Ocular complications of systemic medications	
Medication	Ocular Complications
Amiodarone	Superficial keratopathy
Chlorpromazine	Anterior subcapsular cataracts
Corticosteroids	Posterior subcapsular cataracts, glaucoma
Digitalis	Blurred vision, disturbed color vision
Ethambutol	Optic neuropathy
Indomethacin	Superficial keratopathy
Isoniazid	Optic neuropathy
Nalidixic acid	Papilledema
Hydroxychloroquine	Superficial keratopathy and bull's-eye maculopathy
Tetracycline	Papilledema
Thioridazine	Pigmentary degeneration of the retina
Vitamin A	Papilledema

Appendix D
1. Differential Diagnosis of the Nontraumatic Red Eye

Feature	CONDITION		
	Acute Conjunctivitis	**Acute Iritis**	**Acute Glaucoma**
Symptoms	Redness, tearing +/- discharge	Redness, pain, photophobia	Redness, severe pain, nausea, vomiting
Appearance	Conjunctival injection	Ciliary injection	Diffuse injection
Vision	Normal, can be blurred secondary to discharge	Moderate reduction	Marked reduction, halo vision
Cornea	Clear	May see keratic precipitates	Hazy secondary to edema
Pupil	Normal	Small, sluggish to light	Semidilated, nonreactive
Secretions	Tearing to purulent	Tearing	Tearing
Test & Comments	Smears may show etiology: bacterial infection=polycytes, bacteria; viral infection=monocytes; allergy=eosinophils	Slit lamp will show cells and flare in the anterior chamber	Elevated intraocular pressure
Treatment	Antibiotic	Steroids, cycloplegics	Pilocarpine, Betagan™ Diamox™, mannitol, laser surgery

2. Differential diagnosis of viral, bacterial, and allergic conjunctivitis

Feature	Viral	Bacterial	Allergy
Discharge	Watery	Purulent	Watery
Itching	Minimal	Minimal	Marked
Preauricular lymph node	Common	Absent	Absent
Stain & smear	Monocytes Lymphocytes	Bacteria Polycytes	Eosinophils

Appendix E
Differential Diagnosis of the red eye in contact lens wearers

Diagnosis	Findings	Mechanism	Treatment
Corneal abrasion	Epithelial defect Stains with fluorescein.	Mechanical Hypoxia.	Antibiotic drops (e.g., tobramycin)
Superficial punctate keratitis	Punctate corneal staining	Mechanical. Chemical toxicity	Artificial tears (e.g., Refresh™ ocular lubricant)
Giant papillary conjunctivitis	Papillary reaction of superior tarsal conjunctiva	Immunologic. Mechanical	Mast cell stabilizer (e.g., Vistacrom drops)
Sterile infiltrates	Corneal infiltrate. Epithelium usually intact	Immunologic	Antibiotic drops (assume infected)
Infected ulcer	Corneal infiltrate with ulceration. Stains with fluorescein	Infection (e.g., *Pseudomonas, Staphylococcus aureus)*	Corneal scraping for Gram's stain and cluture. Fortified antibiotic drops